WITHDRAWN

VOICES FROM AROUND THE WORLD

PACIFIC ISLANDS

HAWAI'I

WITHDRAWN

Written by Trisha Kēhaulani Watson-Sproat, J.D., Ph.D.
and Matthew Kawaiola Sproat

NORWOODHOUSE PRESS

Norwood House Press

For more information about Norwood House Press please visit our website at
www.norwoodhousepress.com or call 866-565-2900.

© 2023 Norwood House Press.
All rights reserved. No part of this book may be reproduced or utilized in any form
or by any means without written permission from the publisher.

Credits

Editor: Mari Bolte
Designer: Sara Radka

Photo Credits

Bernice Pauahi Bishop Museum: Cliff, 41, Depositphotos: DeborahKolb, cover, Getty Images: Art Wager, cover, BackyardProduction, 24, bonchan, 39, Dimitris M. Stephanides, 5, Ed Freeman, 44, Eric Broder Van Dyke, 25, Gerald Corsi, cover, insjoy, 26, Kevin Schafer, 42, Maridav, 43, ShaneMyersPhoto, 45, show999, 37, theartist312, 22, Veaceslav Cernat, 29, Hawaii State Archives: 29, Kalihi Palama Culture and Arts Society: James Kimo Garrett, 33, Library of Congress: Charles William Bartlett, 13, Matt Sproat: 34, Newscom: Douglas Peebles, 35, Zak Noyle, 10, Shutterstock: Everett Collection, 17, grebeshkovmaxim, 3, icemanphotos, 5, Maridav, 4, Martina Pellecchia, 31, Peter Hermes Furian, 5, Sahani Photography, 12, Theodore Trimmer, 7, Yi-Chen Chiang, 36, Thompson Publishing Co: Our Islands and Their People, 23, Trisha Kēhaulani Watson-Sproat: , 21, 31, 38, Wellcome Collection: 15, Wikimedia: Allanbcool, 32, aspar Whitney, 27, Bishop Museum, 16, Charles Wickliffe Baldwin, 28, Daniel Ramirez, 40, Hawaii State Archives, 19, Hawaii Territory Survey, 11, John Webber, 9, Mark James Miller, 18, Thomas Tunsch, 30, Unknown, 14

Library of Congress Cataloging-in-Publication Data

Library of Congress Cataloging-in-Publication Data has been filed and is available at catalog.loc.gov

Hardcover ISBN: 978-1-68450-749-8
Paperback ISBN: 978-1-68404-812-0

Table of Contents

GUIDE TO HAWAIIAN PRONUNCIATION

The Hawaiian language has two diacritical markings, the 'okina and the kahakō.

The 'okina is a glottal stop. This means it is made by closing the vocal cords, or glottis, while speaking. When used, it occurs when one syllable ends and the next begins. The sound is similar to the sound made while saying "oh-oh." It is shown as '. It is considered its own letter of the Hawaiian alphabet. It always precedes a vowel and never precedes a consonant. There are never two 'okina used in a row.

The kahakō is a mark used to show a long or stressed vowel. It is shown as a line above a letter, like ō. The use or location of an 'okina and kahakō can change the meaning of a word.

Welcome to Hawai'i

Aloha! This commonly used term is often heard throughout the Hawaiian Islands. It is generally a warm expression, greeting, or salutation.

Aloha is known to have many meanings. It is most commonly a way to show respect, appreciation, and love. Aloha is also an attitude. This is where the term "the aloha spirit" comes from. One who acts with aloha is said to be caring and considerate. When we show aloha for one another, we treat one another with kindness and respect.

In Hawai'i, people are given *lei* (garlands) for special occasions. Lei can be made or purchased at lei stands around the islands.

Expressions of aloha go beyond our treatment of each other. Having the aloha spirit also means to have aloha for the land, environment, and all living beings.

Where is Hawai'i?

Hawai'i is in the North Pacific Ocean. It's an expansive **archipelago** extending across 1,500 miles (2,414 kilometers). The eight main islands are Hawai'i, Maui, Moloka'i, O'ahu, Kaua'i, Kaho'olawe, Lāna'i, and Ni'ihau.

Kaua'i

Ni'ihau

PACIFIC OCEAN

O'ahu

Honolulu

Moloka'i

Lāna'i

Maui

Kaho'olawe

PACIFIC OCEAN

Hawai'i

The capital, Honolulu, is on O'ahu.

CHAPTER 1

The History of Hawai'i

Hawaiians have many origin stories. Some spoke of the world beginning in Hawai'i. Others told of great travelers who settled the islands.

One of these creation stories is the *Kumulipo*. It is a chant shared in *'ōlelo Hawai'i* (Hawaiian language). In written form, it is longer than 2,100 lines. It can take many hours to recite.

At first, the universe was dark. The chant describes the night. Then, two gods were born. One was Kumulipo, a male. The other was Po'ele, a female. It was then that the day began. This chant continues to recount the birth of the islands, humans, and many of the species found in the islands.

This creation story also traces the lineage of a family of chiefs dating back to the birth of the gods. It ties *kānaka* (Native Hawaiians) to the *'āina* (land).

Shown to the right, Princess Bernice Pauahi Bishop (1831–1884) descended from a long line of chiefs.

Who is "Hawaiian"?

In Hawai'i, the term "Hawaiian" means that one is Native Hawaiian. This term is for people who are lineal descendants of the people who inhabited the Hawaiian Islands prior to the arrival of Europeans in 1776. If you live in Hawai'i but are not of Native Hawaiian descent, you are referred to as a "Hawai'i Resident" or "local." However, you are not called or considered "Hawaiian."

One migration story tells of a fisherman named Hawai'iloa. He came across the islands during a long trip at sea. The islands were named after himself and his children. He used the stars to find his way home. Then, he brought his family back to the islands. In this history, all Hawaiian people trace their lineages back to him.

Experts believe the first people settled in Hawai'i around 400 CE, or about 1,600 years ago. They traveled north from the Marquesas Islands. The islands are about 2,000 miles (3,219 km) south of Hawai'i.

Double-hulled voyaging canoes brought people across the ocean. Sails were woven from coconut fronds or pandanus tree leaves. Large oars were used to steer. The voyages were not easy. Storms could destroy a canoe. The process for selecting the right tree for building a canoe was a sacred process

Wa'a (canoes) were used for traveling between the islands.

The early voyagers did not have modern tools to help them find their way. It took years for master navigators to learn their craft. They used things like waves, clouds, stars, and birds to navigate over long distances. Younger sailors studied under older masters to develop their skills. They were taught about the oceans and the stars.

The first people who traveled to Hawaiʻi knew a lot about the natural world. They used traditional science and engineering to settle the islands. They grew a thriving, independent community. It is estimated that as many as one million people lived in Hawaiʻi before Western contact.

Settling the Seas

Pacific Islanders traveled over an area more than 10 million square miles (26 million square kilometers). By the time European explorers ventured to the same areas in the 1500s, island settlers had already been there for hundreds of years.

A modern-day double hulled canoe called *Hōkūleʻa* traveled the world from 2013 to 2017. Its team used traditional navigation tools.

Hōkūleʻa was built to bring awareness to the importance of caring for our Earth and oceans.

Hawaii's society was complex. The islands were ruled by *ali'i* (chiefs). These chiefs were believed to be descendants of the gods. The ali'i had advisers who guided them. Together, they managed the islands.

Chiefs were able to manage large land areas through the *ahupua'a* system. This was a traditional land division. It ran from the top of a mountain ridge out to the ocean reef. It was similar to how water runs from a high point to a low point.

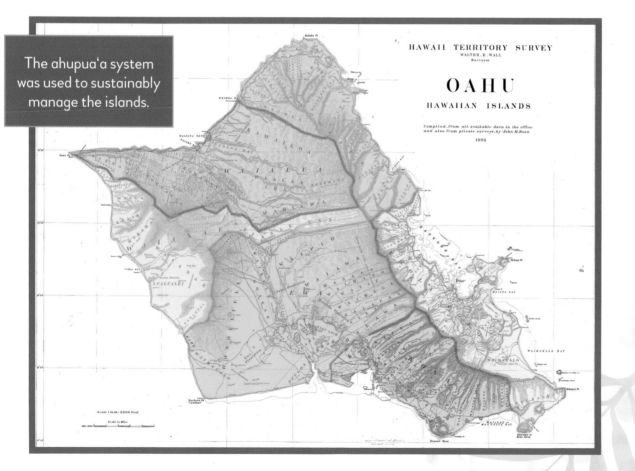

The ahupua'a system was used to sustainably manage the islands.

Hawaiians gathered and caught their own food. They knew their home well. A wide range of skills allowed them to thrive. Hawaiians lived with their extended families in clusters of houses or small family villages. Everyone pitched in to do their parts.

Many people were farmers. Hawaiians used fresh water from streams to feed *loʻi* (pond fields). Loʻi were found across the islands. The most common food crop to grow in loʻi was taro. It was a staple food source for Hawaiians. *Poi* (cooked and pounded taro), sweet potato, *laulau* (pork with fish wrapped in taro leaves), and *haupia* (coconut pudding) are foods still found at meals today.

Taro farming still occurs throughout the islands. These large taro fields can be found on Kauaʻi.

Fishermen used their knowledge of the seas to feed their families and communities.

Hawaiians were also expert fishermen. They fished in both the deep sea and in the shallow coastal areas. Some traditional techniques required many people to work together. They would pull large nets to shore, gathering enough food for everyone.

Hawaiians have records of their history over hundreds of years. Many involve great leaders. The most important of these chiefs is Kamehameha.

Kamehameha was born around 1758 on the Island of Hawai'i. He was the son and grandson of great chiefs. There were signs or prophecies before his birth that said he would become a great king. These prophecies came true. After years of fighting and talking, Kamehameha was able to unite all of the Hawaiian Islands.

By 1810, all the Hawaiian Islands were unified under Kamehameha's rule.

Europeans would not arrive in the Hawaiians Islands until 1778. The English explorer Captain James Cook first landed in Waimea, on the island of Kaua'i. At first, Hawaiians were fascinated with the foreigners. But their arrival would have consequences.

Native Hawaiians had not been exposed to foreign diseases before. Their bodies did not know how to fight them off. Chicken pox, polio, measles, and tuberculosis spread across the islands. Experts believe the original population in 1778 was between 300,000 and 700,000. By 1920, there were fewer than 24,000 Native Hawaiians left.

Captain Cook (center) called the Hawaiian Islands the Sandwich Islands, to honor the 4th Earl of Sandwich. The Earl had funded Cook's journey.

Hawaiian Newspapers

The first Christian **missionaries** arrived on the island in 1820. The missionaries brought religion, the written word, and the printing press with them. They taught Hawaiians how to read and write. The first Hawaiian language newspaper was published in 1834 on the Island of Maui. By the mid-1800s, Native Hawaiians were among the most **literate** population in the world. There were more than 100 different newspapers in the Hawaiian language. These newspapers exist today as the world's largest native language collection.

After Kamehameha formed the modern Kingdom of Hawai'i, changes to the government were made. One of the biggest changes was related to land ownership.

Traditionally, Hawaiians lived in harmony with the land. They served as its caretakers. Chiefs helped manage the land and natural resources. Rules, known as the *kapu* system, were in place. They were to protect the land and ocean from being used up. Everyone got a share of what was grown or produced.

Kamehameha's son was Kauikeaouli, also known as Kamehameha III. He knew foreigners wanted his people's land. In 1848, he passed an act called the Māhele. It divided the land and let private owners control property. The native people wanted to retain family lands. But property ownership was a new concept. The process of applying for and receiving land benefitted foreigners. Many Hawaiians lost their lands.

Kamehameha III

Farm laborers were needed to work on plantations.

The Māhele allowed the foreigners to snatch up large chunks of land. They built huge sugar and pineapple **plantations**. They drilled water wells and took fresh water from natural streams to feed their thirsty crops. Plantation owners also brought workers in from Europe and Asia.

Foreign greed and desire for Hawaii's resources grew throughout the 1800s. Plantation owners were attracted to Hawaii's fresh water and large areas of land. The sugar industry created a different way of life. Most of the plantation owners were powerful American businessmen. The Kingdom of Hawaiʻi and its rulers worked hard to make sure Hawaiians and immigrant workers were treated fairly.

Hawaiians were aware of America's past of enslaving Africans and slaughtering native people. The **monarchy** passed a law in 1852 banning slavery. They also declared that any slave brought to Hawaiʻi would be immediately freed.

American and European businessmen did not like the Hawaiian leadership. They worked against the native government for years. In 1881, the king at the time, David Kalākaua, died. His sister, Queen Liliʻuokalani, would take the throne. She worked to pass new laws. They would give her people more rights.

Queen Liliʻuokalani

In January of 1893, a group of angry businessmen met. They threatened violence against the Kingdom and the queen. They were supported by American troops. To avoid conflict and death, the queen yielded her authority to the United States. The businessmen made themselves the new temporary government.

American troops occupied Queen Lili'uokalani's palace.

In 1900, Hawai'i became a territory of the United States. This was good for wealthy landowners but bad for everyone else. For nearly 60 years, people, many of them American, worked to make Hawai'i a state. In 1959, Hawai'i would become the 50th state of America.

DID YOU KNOW?

The first Black person to move to Hawai'i was Anthony D. Allen. He was a freedman who traveled the world until settling in Hawai'i in 1810. He worked as a steward to King Kamehameha.

CHAPTER 2
Life in the Islands

The Hawaiian islands were created over millions of years. Each is made up of at least one volcano. Some of those volcanoes are still active. Kīlauea, on the Island of Hawai'i, has been continuously erupting since 1983.

Many of Hawaii's volcanoes have become large mountains. Mauna Kea is one of these large mountains. Located on the Island of Hawai'i, its base is deep under the Pacific Ocean. From the base to the peak, Mauna Kea stands more than 33,500 feet (10,210 meters) high. Snow falls on the top of its peaks.

People think of Hawai'i as a tropical retreat. But it has many climates. There are 14 different climate zones in the world, and Hawai'i is home to 10 of them. The tropical weather and remote location has made the land and water rich in **biodiversity**. Many native plants and birds live and grow here. Volcanoes and mountains stretch into the clouds. Forests and beaches can be seen for miles. The peak of Mauna Kea can reach temperatures below freezing.

Great efforts are taken to protect threatened and endangered species. This land snail is highly endangered.

DID YOU KNOW?

Foreigners valued Hawaii's natural resources, but they did not care for the land. Thousands of native species have gone extinct. Hundreds more are threatened or endangered. Today, Hawai'i is considered the "endangered species capital of the world."

Kīlauea Volcano is said to be the home of the fire goddess Pele.

Hawaiians were very aware of the natural world. They understood that their survival was tied to the health of the environment around them. They were always very careful to respect the land and water.

Kānaka believed that all beings had value. Many of the living things around them were thought to be extensions of the gods. For example, the ocean god Kanaloa was said to take the form of an octopus. He could also take the form of foods, like bananas. All the traditional Hawaiian gods had many forms.

These traditions were shared as *moʻolelo* (histories or stories told out loud). They helped the people stay connected to and understand their past. Moʻolelo contained a rich body of knowledge. They were passed down from one generation to the next. Many Hawaiian children grew up hearing and learning moʻolelo from their grandparents and parents. Other family members and teachers had their own lessons.

Mele and Hula (Song and Dance)

Hawaiian songs are called *mele*. Mele have been written for hundreds of years. Before the introduction of modern instruments, Hawaiians composed *ʻoli* (chants) that celebrated people and places.

Hula refers to Hawaiian dance. There are millions of hula dances across the globe. Traditional hula, performed without modern musical instruments, is called *hula kahiko*. Modern hula, which is accompanied by music with instruments like guitars, pianos, or ukulele, is referred to as *hula ʻauana*.

Hula and mele have a long history in the islands.

Located on Kaua'i, Alakoko Fishpond is over 100 acres (40.5 hectares) in size. It is actively being restored and preserved by the community.

Hawaiians were master engineers. They built large fishponds through a technique of drystone **masonry**. Passing on this skill was very important. Many generations could build and maintain these traditional Hawaiian fishpond systems.

There were once more than 400 traditional fishponds across Hawai'i. The ones that still exist today are hundreds of years old. They were used for **aquaculture**. Fish, shellfish, seaweed, and other edible items were grown. These fishponds were important. They helped to feed people in the communities.

Hawaiians used many engineering methods to build and keep these fishponds. The fishponds used the fresh water that flowed from the uplands. Then, it was mixed with ocean water. This created slightly salty water. Young fish would find the ponds. Gates allowed the small fish to swim in. The fish would happily feed in the pond and grow. Once they were mature, they would be too large to fit through the gates. They could be easily harvested for food.

Traditional Religious Sites

Drystack masonry was also used to build large temples. Aliʻi would take time to select the right location. There were different types of temples, and building one was a deeply spiritual endeavor. Many cultural protocols were followed. There were once hundreds that existed across Hawaiʻi. Many of these sites have been destroyed as a result of modernity, but the ones that remain can still be found today.

Drystack masonry does not use concrete.

The people who immigrated to Hawaiʻi had their own customs, foods, and traditions. They built schools and stores. The many groups needed a common language. A **pidgin** language developed. It is also known as Hawaiʻi Creole English. It's mainly English, but it includes words from other languages, like Hawaiian, Chinese, Portuguese, and Japanese.

Many early Hawaiian foods are still enjoyed. But Asian cultures brought their own dishes. One example is short grain rice. This tasty, sticky starch is the main side served today.

Manapua, a dish inspired by the Chinese bao, has been widely enjoyed throughout the islands for decades.

The Lūʻau Tradition

Traditionally, Hawaiian men and women did not eat together. This custom was changed by King Liholiho, also known as Kamehameha II. After Liholiho passed away, his younger brother succeeded him. Kamehameha III threw grand feasts that would come to be known as *lūʻau*. Today, lūʻau are still commonly held for family celebrations, including weddings, graduation parties, and other significant events. The most important lūʻau a family holds is in celebration of a baby's first birthday.

Royal lūʻau were grand celebrations.

Another example is Chinese *bao*. Bao are steamed or baked buns with a meat filling. The Hawaiians would call this *mea ʻono puaʻa*, or a delicious pork pastry. This would be shortened to *manapua*. Manapua can be found throughout the islands today.

Japanese food would also have a huge influence on Hawaii's local flavor. Japanese teriyaki can be widely found in local restaurants. This technique involves cooking foods with soy sauce, called by its Japanese name, shoyu.

In 1793, British Captain George Vancouver gave cattle to King Kamehameha. This was the first introduction of cattle to the Hawaiian Islands. Vancouver thought they could be used to trade in the future.

For the next 30 years, Kamehameha placed a kapu on the cattle. No one was allowed to harm them. They were allowed to roam the hillsides. The cattle bred in great numbers. While this was good for trade, it was not good for the land. Many cultural sites and resources were trampled.

Cattle have been in Hawai'i since the late 18th century. Rodeos are still held in Hawai'i today.

In 1823, Kamehameha III wanted to control the cattle. He invited Mexican cowboys, called vaqueros, to Hawai'i. They would teach the Hawaiians how to rope, ride, and become cowboys.

DID YOU KNOW?

The first cowboys in America were the Hawaiian paniolo. They were roping cows and riding horses before the Wild West cowboy culture emerged.

The Spanish vaqueros were called "españoles," or "Spanish people." However, Hawaiians could not pronounce the word. Instead, the name became "paniolo." From that point, anyone in Hawai'i who cared and worked with cattle were paniolo.

Horses were first brought to the Islands in 1803.

Slack Key Guitar

Españoles brought the Spanish guitar with them to the islands. After their long workdays, they would play guitars and sing of their homeland. Many eventually returned to Mexico. When they left, they gave their guitars to their paniolo friends. The paniolo did not know how to tune the instruments, so they would "slack" the strings to create sounds they thought were pretty. After a few years of mastering this technique, the Hawaiian "slack key guitar" became a unique style of tuning and playing. Today, this style of guitar playing has a global audience.

Traditional practices, like making bark cloth, continue throughout the island. Bark cloth fabric was used as clothing and is used still in hula today.

Cultural traditions in Hawai'i today are inspired by their heritage and nature. Hula and music are two examples. But many more still take place. Others are growing in practice.

Foreigners, and especially missionaries, worked hard to get Native Hawaiians to turn to Christianity. Part of this effort included cutting out the Hawaiian way of life. Traditional beliefs, culture, customs, and practices were stopped or even lost. This spread even farther after the Kingdom fell. The Western government made many cultural practices forbidden. They even banned speaking Hawaiian. Children were punished in school for speaking it.

Throughout the 20th century, many Hawaiian practices were done in secret. Elders would teach customs to their family members. In this way, they could help preserve the culture. In the 1970s, a Hawaiian Renaissance emerged. Hawaiians were finally allowed and encouraged to return to their traditional practices.

Elders keep customs and traditions alive.

Printed Tradition

Like in other parts of Polynesia, tattoos are part of the culture. Getting a tattoo can be an important life event for young Native Hawaiians. Traditional tattooing tools, including needles, are made from bird bones. For many people, the first traditional tattoo runs from ankle to hip. Master practitioners design tattoos based on an individual's family line. Every design is unique to the person receiving it. Receiving a traditional tattoo can be a very sacred process and is done in ceremony.

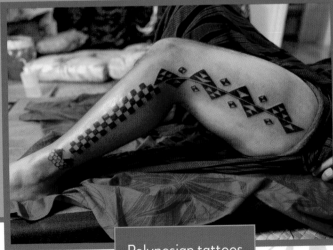

Polynesian tattoos are a form of art.

CHAPTER 3

Island Celebrations

Celebrations and festivals honor the traditions of people of the past. Hawai'i is rich with cultural diversity. Migrants from across the world moved to Hawai'i over the last 200 years. This created a unique community. Cultural and ethnic identities blended.

Restoration Day and Independence Day both date back to the Kingdom of Hawai'i. But other celebrations are rooted in the Hawaiian culture.

The Merrie Monarch Hula Festival's three-day competition is world-famous.

Some hula schools accept students as young as 3 years old. Many students stay with the same school for years.

The Merrie Monarch Hula Festival is considered the Olympics of Hula. This weeklong festival was started in 1964. It praises King David Kalākaua's efforts to bring back the Hawaiian culture, specifically hula. It is held in Hilo during the week following Easter. There is also a large market, the world's biggest and best hula competition, and a parade. People come from around the world to attend this honored celebration.

The Queen Liliʻuokalani Keiki Hula Competition honors the queen's love of children. Hundreds of young people participate every year.

Another popular celebration is May Day. May Day is also known as Lei Day in Hawai'i. It was first celebrated in 1927. The next year, the first Lei Queen was crowned. A Lei Day court is chosen. They oversee Lei Day celebrations. They also represent their community during events throughout the year. Lei makers compete in contests to show off elaborate creations.

People share lei with loved ones.

King Kamehameha I is recognized each year on June 11. In 1871, Kamehameha V decided to honor his great-grandfather. This is the only holiday declared by royalty and still officially observed. There are parades and hula dancing. Thousands of people attend. Three statues of Kamehameha stand in Hawai'i. Ceremonies take place at each of them. The statues are draped in many lei. This is a grand celebration.

While a lei-draping ceremony takes place on Kamehameha Day, lei can be made and worn every day. They are mostly worn around the neck. But lei can also be worn around the head. They can be made from many different materials. Flowers are the most common. But they can also be made from shells or feathers. Some lei are strung together. Others are braided or woven.

Adorning Kamehameha statues with hundreds of lei is a tradition for Kamehameha Day.

Language Lesson

Hawai'i has two official languages: Hawaiian and English. Hawaiian is its own unique language, but it is often **anglicized**. Generally, diacritical markings are not used in anglicized words. For example, "Hawaiian" is an anglicized word, so there is not an 'okina.

Similarly, the plural form of Hawaiian words typically use kahakō. Instead of adding an "s", plural words have "nā" in front of them. The word for *woman* is *wāhine*, but "women" would be *nā wāhine*. The word for *man* is *kane*, but "men" is spelled *nā kāne*.

Chinese Lion Dance teams perform at festivals, parades, and other celebrations.

Foreign diseases led to huge drops in the Native Hawaiian population. Business owners needed workers for their plantations. They looked overseas. They first brought immigrants from China and Portugal. Workers from Japan, Puerto Rico, and Korea followed. There were also Spanish and Filipino workers.

Chinese New Year is based on the lunar calendar. It is widely celebrated among the large Chinese population on the islands. Many Chinese traditions are kept alive. People eat special foods. They attend lion dances, which are said to keep away evil spirits. Fireworks are set off to drive away spirits and cleanse the home.

Many Japanese and other Asian dates are also observed. Girls' Day is March 3. Boys' Day or Children's Day is May 5. Children are the center of attention on these days. Obon festivals and bon dances are also very popular. These come from a Buddhist custom of honoring one's ancestors. The obon season lasts from June to September. There are dances every weekend. They also include a traditional Japanese dance called Bon Odori.

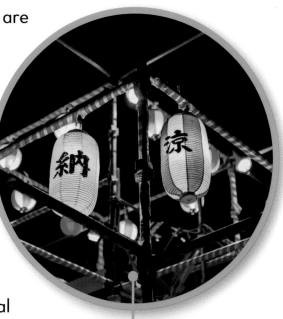

Traditional lanterns are an important part of Obon festivals.

Cultural Authenticity

Customs are beautiful and captivating. They are also the unique innovations of different cultural groups from around the world. In an increasingly globalized world, many of these cultural practices, ideas, and words become misappropriated. This is when another person or group takes a cultural invention that is not theirs and claims it as their own. This is wrong and very hurtful to indigenous people and other cultural communities. It is very important to promote cultural authenticity by supporting legitimate cultural practitioners.

CHAPTER 4

Hawai'i Today

Today, there more than 1.4 million people living in the islands. Around 300,000 are Native Hawaiians. It is one of the most racially diverse places on Earth. As many as 11 million people visit each year for work or fun.

Passionfruit, called *liliko'i* in Hawaiian, was brought to Hawai'i in the late 1800s.

Daytime temperatures are pleasant year-round. They range from 78 degrees to 84 degrees Fahrenheit (25.5 to 29 degrees Celsius). The mountains and wind work together. This creates rainy conditions. East-facing sides of the islands have higher rainfall than west sides. As a result, the eastern slopes are lush. Hawaii's tropical weather means fresh fruits can be enjoyed throughout the year. Passionfruit and bananas are favorites. Guava and papaya are others.

Poke!

Poke means "to cut or slice" in Hawaiian. It is a method of fish cutting. It is also a Hawaiian dish. Poke is a fusion dish. It combines this Hawaiian method of cutting raw fish with native or Asian ingredients, typically shoyu or sriracha. Poke bowls include local poke over steamed short-grain rice. You can buy poke or poke bowls at local grocery stores. Locals will tell you this uniquely Hawai'i dish is *'ono* (delicious)! It's the perfect dish to bring to a potluck as *pūpū* (appetizer).

The literal translation of poke is "cut into chunks." It is pronounced POH-kay.

For most of Hawaii's history, Hawaiian was the main language. **Globalization** would bring more people. Those people brought their cultures and languages. At least 130 other different languages are now also heard around the islands. One-quarter of all people in Hawai'i speak another language at home. Tagalog, Ilocano, and Japanese are the top three.

Different cultures and traditions are celebrated throughout Hawai'i.

A Melting Pot

Diversity is beautiful. Just ask the people of Hawai'i. People from all different ethnic backgrounds and heritages have long lived among each other in these islands. As a result, people from different ethnic backgrounds commonly married and had families. The result is that many of the people who live in Hawai'i today have a mix of ethnicities.

The first public education system dates back to 1840. It was founded by King Kamehameha III. It is the oldest educational system west of the Mississippi River. Today, there are both public and private schools.

Punahou is a private school on Oʻahu. It opened in 1842. The school has a long history of famous students. Some include Prince Kūhiō, former president Barack Obama, and Olympian Carissa Moore. Princess Bernice Pauahi had an estate of more than 375,000 acres (151,757 hectares) of land. When she died, she gifted that land. It was to build Kamehameha Schools, a school for Native Hawaiian children. There are also two- and four-year colleges and universities for students who want to pursue higher education.

Bishop Museum served as the original location for the Kamehameha Schools for Boys. The school built a new campus in 1940. The school continues to operate as a museum and is open to the public today.

When non-islanders think of Hawaiʻi, they probably think of lūʻau, lei, kalua pork, and surfing. Hawaiʻi has long been seen as a vacation spot. But this means the idea of local culture is sometimes manipulated. Figuring out what's true culture and what's fiction can be difficult. Hotels, golf courses, and other places of interest have taken over historic or cultural sites in an effort to preserve Hawaii's true culture.

People are becoming more culturally and environmentally aware. Hawaiians have taken leadership roles in tourism. They want to educate visitors. Honoring locations like burial grounds, coral reefs, and nesting sites for endangered species is important. Additionally, authentic dishes made with taro and other traditional foods are replacing commercialized foods such as pineapple pizza.

Visitors to the islands should come willing to share in the aloha spirit. They should treat the islands and its people with respect. If you do these things, you will be welcomed by the island people and truly enjoy your time in Hawaiʻi.

Hawaiian monk seals are only found on the Hawaiian Islands.

Hiking in Hawai'i allows visitors a look at the unique landscape and cultural history.

Visiting Respectfully

Treating a new place with respect is important. Hawai'i has many beautiful sites, but some of these can include dangerous activities and can be unsafe. Do not trespass. Do not wander off marked areas or trails. Be careful when you go swimming! Hawaii's currents are strong and can easily sweep you out to sea. Do not step on coral or reefs. Keep a safe distance from wildlife. The best trip is a safe trip.

Hawai'i has a rich history. The beauty of Hawai'i comes from not only its natural resources but its diverse cultures. The Native Hawaiian people have always been welcoming, and that has grown into a population that truly lives the aloha spirit on a daily basis.

It is important that we all work to keep Hawai'i as unique and beautiful as it has been for hundreds of years. Over-development poses a real threat to Hawai'i and its people. The high cost of living has forced many Native Hawaiian families to leave their homeland to find affordable places to live. There is no Hawai'i without Native Hawaiians. It is the native people who are the heart and soul of these islands.

Farmer's markets let people find and try produce and ingredients only found on the islands.

Oahu's North Shore is known for its beauty.

A Hawaiian **proverb** says, "He aliʻi ka ʻāina, he kauwā ke kānaka." This means, "The land is a chief, and man is its servant." Whether you travel to Hawaiʻi or explore places closer to home, it is important to remember that nature and the people must work in harmony.

Hawaiian Glossary

Remember to check page 3 for tips on pronunciation!

ahupua'a: a traditional system of land division

'āina: land

ali'i: chiefs

aloha: love; also used as a greeting

haupia: coconut pudding

hula: dance

hula 'auana: modern hula

hula kahiko: traditional hula

kānaka: Native Hawaiians

kane: man; plural form is nā kāne

kapu: a system of rules used for management

laulau: pork with fish wrapped in taro leaves

lei: garlands

liliko'i: passionfruit

lo'i: pond fields

lū'au: feasts

mea 'ono pua'a: delicious pork pastry; also shorted to manapua

mele: songs

mo'olelo: histories or stories told out loud

'ōlelo Hawai'i: Hawaiian language

'oli: chants

'ono: delicious

poi: cooked and pounded taro

poke: to cut or slice; a dish made with fish

pūpū: appetizer

wa'a: canoes

wāhine: woman; plural form is nā wāhine

English Glossary

anglicized (AEN-gluh-syzd): to adapt a foreign word for English use

aquaculture (AK-wuh-kult-shuhr): raising animals or plants that live or grow in the water for food

archipelago (ahr-kuh-PEL-uh-go): an island, or group of islands

biodiversity (by-oh-dye-VER-suh-tee): the variety of life in a particular area

globalization (gloh-buh-lye-ZAY-shuhn): the connection and interdependence of economies, cultures, and populations

literate (LIT-uh-ruht): able to read and write

masonry (MAY-suhn-ree): stonework

missionaries (MISH-uh-nehr-ees): people sent to promote Christianity in a foreign country

monarchy (MAH-nar-kee): a form of government in which a leader rules for life

pidgin (PID-jin): a simplified form of communication used by people who don't share a common language

plantations (plan-TAY-shuhns): large farms or estates that grow crops to sell or make a profit

proverb (PROH-vuhrb): a short saying that gives advice or explains some truth about life

Read More about the Pacific Islands

Books

Loh-Hagan, Virginia. *Colonization of Hawaiʻi*. Ann Arbor, MI: Cherry Lake Publishing, 2022.

Serrano, Christy. *The Attack on Pearl Harbor: A Day that Changed America*. North Mankato, MN: Capstone Press, an imprint of Capstone, 2022.

Vaʻafusuaga, Jane. *Sāmoa*. Chicago, IL: Norwood House Press, 2023.

Websites

Hawaiian Electronic Library (http://ulukau.org) An extensive online collection of Hawaiian cultural resources.

Hawaiian Language Dictionary (http://www.wehewehe.org) A dictionary in both the Hawaiian language and in English.

Hawaiʻi State Public Library System: Learn about Hawaiian History (https://www.librarieshawaii.org/2021/09/03/learn-about-hawaiian-history/) The Hawaiʻi State Public Library System highlights reading resources.

Mālama Hawaiʻi (https://www.gohawaii.com/malama) The Hawaiʻi Tourism Authority has information about culture and natural resources.

Index

About the Authors

Matthew Kawaiola Sproat and Trisha Kēhaulani Watson-Sproat are husband and wife. They are both Native Hawaiian and both born and raised on the Island of O'ahu. Today, they live with their family in Honolulu (Kaimukī).

Matt is an award-winning traditional Hawaiian musician, having played with his group Waipuna in venues across the world. He is also a celebrated master woodworker through his company, The Kealohi Collection.

Kēhau was the first Native Hawaiian woman to obtain two doctorate degrees. She has both a law degree and a Ph.D. Kēhau is an expert in historic preservation, conservation, and traditional ecological knowledge. Her company, Honua Consulting, is Hawaii's largest Native Hawaiian-owned cultural resource management company.

A portion of book proceeds will go to the Queen Lili'uokalani Keiki Hula Competition. To learn more about this event, visit http://www.keikihula.org.

CONTRA COSTA COUNTY LIBRARY

31901069003889